HOTTEST HABITATS

BY ASHLEY GISH

Apex is distributed by North Star Editions:
sales@northstareditions.com | 888-417-0195

Produced for Apex by Red Line Editorial.

Photographs ©: Shutterstock Images, cover, 1, 4–5, 6, 7, 8–9, 12, 14, 18, 18–19, 21, 29; iStockphoto, 10–11, 16–17, 20; Rick & Nora Bowers/Alamy, 15; P. Rona/OAR/NURP/NOAA, 22–23; AD Rogers, PA Tyler, DP Connelly, JT Copley, R James, et al./Public Library of Science/ Public Library of Science, 24; NOAA OKEANOS Explorer Program/NOAA, 25; David Shale/ NaturePL/Science Source, 26; OER/OAR/NOAA, 27

Library of Congress Control Number: 2022919882

ISBN
978-1-63738-530-2 (hardcover)
978-1-63738-584-5 (paperback)
978-1-63738-691-0 (ebook pdf)
978-1-63738-638-5 (hosted ebook)

Printed in the United States of America
Mankato, MN
082023

NOTE TO PARENTS AND EDUCATORS

Apex books are designed to build literacy skills in striving readers. Exciting, high-interest content attracts and holds readers' attention. The text is carefully leveled to allow students to achieve success quickly. Additional features, such as bolded glossary words for difficult terms, help build comprehension.

TABLE OF CONTENTS

CHAPTER 1

A HOT MEAL

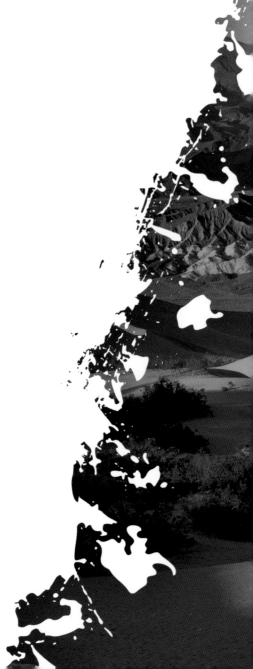

The sun rises over Death Valley's sand **dunes**. It's five o'clock in the morning. But the temperature is already 98 degrees Fahrenheit (37°C).

Horned rattlesnakes have bumps by their eyes. The bumps may help block sand.

A horned rattlesnake is hunting for breakfast. It sees a roadrunner. The snake tries to sneak up on the bird. But it is no match for the bird's quick **reflexes**.

Roadrunners don't fly much. Instead, they run along the ground.

The roadrunner stabs the rattlesnake with its beak. It slams the snake against the ground. Then it eats the snake.

Roadrunners catch and eat snakes, lizards, and more. They often peck their food to kill it.

FAST FACT

Roadrunners don't need to drink. Instead, they get water from their food.

CHAPTER 2

DESERT DWELLERS

Deserts are some of the hottest places on Earth. But many animals have **adapted** to live in them. For example, jerboas live in the Sahara. Large ears help their bodies stay cool.

Dromedary camels can also live in the Sahara. Humps on their backs store fat. Camels can use the fat for energy. They can go months without food.

HIGH FLYERS

Rüppell's vultures live in the **Sahel**. They are some of the highest-flying birds in the world. They soar on warm air that rises high into the sky.

◀ Camels can go days with no food or water. People can use them to travel across deserts.

California leaf-nosed bats live in the Sonoran Desert. They can go up to six weeks without water.

FAST FACT
The Sonoran Desert is one of the hottest places in the world. Iran's Lut Desert is another.

The Sonoran Desert covers parts of the United States and Mexico.

California leaf-nosed bats rest in caves during the day.

CHAPTER 3

KEEPING COOL

Many desert animals are nocturnal. They come out at night when the air is cooler. Sand cats are one example. They sleep in burrows during the day.

Sand cats live in parts of Northern Africa, Central Asia, and the Middle East.

A jackrabbit's huge ears help its body stay cool. They let out heat.

Jackrabbits live in North and Central America. They move most at **dawn** and **dusk**. Rüppell's foxes live in the Lut Desert. They hunt at night.

Rüppell's foxes eat plants and small animals.

FAST FACT

Rüppell's foxes have fur on their foot pads. This helps them not get burned by hot sand.

The desert spadefoot is a type of toad.

Desert spadefoots live in Australia. Temperatures can reach 122 degrees Fahrenheit (50°C). To stay cool, spadefoots bury themselves in the sand. They come out to eat and have babies.

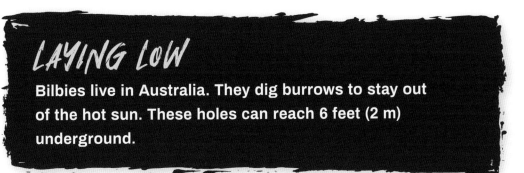

LAYING LOW

Bilbies live in Australia. They dig burrows to stay out of the hot sun. These holes can reach 6 feet (2 m) underground.

Few bilbies are left in the wild. They are in danger of dying out.

CHAPTER 4

DEEP-SEA HEAT

Hydrothermal vents are openings in the seafloor. Hot water comes out of them. Water near the vents can be 750 degrees Fahrenheit (400°C).

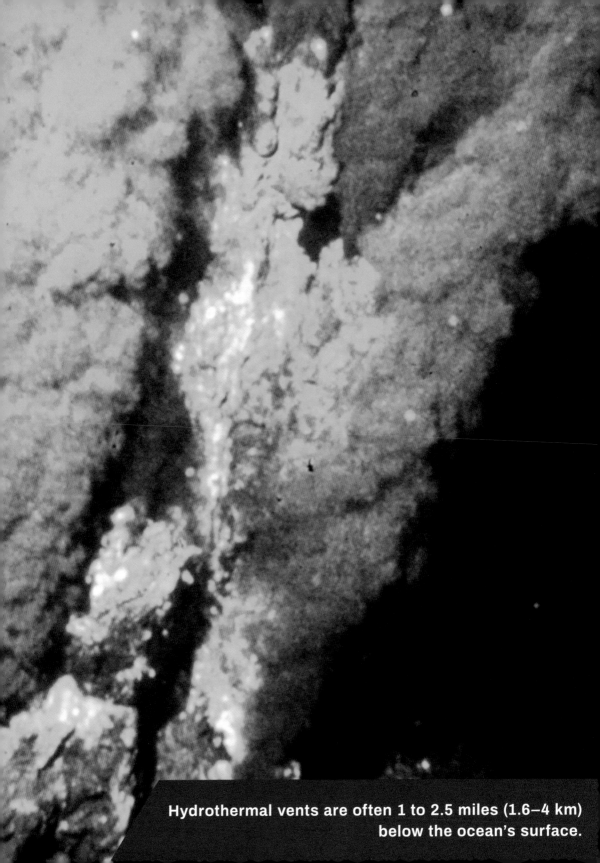

Hydrothermal vents are often 1 to 2.5 miles (1.6–4 km) below the ocean's surface.

Vent octopuses can live more than 9,200 feet (2,800 m) underwater.

Vent octopuses live near hydrothermal vents. They hunt in water that is up to 196 degrees Fahrenheit (91°C). They eat small sea animals.

HOT EGGS

Skates are related to sharks and rays. Pacific white skates lay their eggs next to hydrothermal vents. Warm water helps the eggs hatch more quickly.

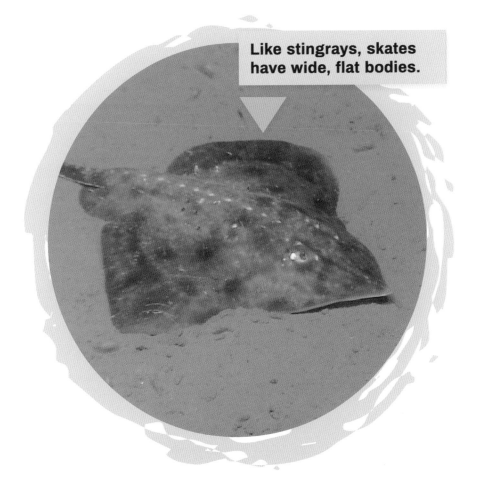

Like stingrays, skates have wide, flat bodies.

Yeti crabs have long, hairy arms. Some hold their arms over hot vents. **Bacteria** grow on the hairs. The crabs may eat the bacteria.

Yeti crabs can grow 6 inches (15 cm) long.

Several types of shrimp and crabs live near hydrothermal vents.

FAST FACT

Yeti crabs have no eyes. They may use their arm hairs to sense.

COMPREHENSION QUESTIONS

Write your answers on a separate piece of paper.

1. Write a few sentences describing the main ideas of Chapter 3.

2. Would you want to live in or near a desert? Why or why not?

3. Which animal grows bacteria on its arms?

    A. desert spadefoot

    B. vent octopus

    C. yeti crab

4. Why would being able to go a long time without food help animals survive in the desert?

    A. No plants or animals live in deserts.

    B. Fewer plants and animals can live in deserts.

    C. Most deserts have too many animals.

5. What does **nocturnal** mean in this book?

*Many desert animals are **nocturnal**. They come out at night when the air is cooler.*

    A. active during the day

    B. active during the night

    C. sleeping all year long

6. What does **burrows** mean in this book?

*They dig **burrows** to stay out of the hot sun. These holes can reach 6 feet (2 m) underground.*

    A. things that animals eat

    B. underground places where animals live

    C. times of year when animals have babies

Answer key on page 32.

GLOSSARY

adapted
Changed to fit a particular situation.

bacteria
Tiny living things.

dawn
The time of day when the sun is starting to rise.

deserts
Areas of land that have few plants and get very little rain.

dunes
Hills of sand formed by wind.

dusk
The time of day just before night when the sky gets dark.

hydrothermal
Relating to hot water.

reflexes
Actions done very quickly, with little or no thinking.

Sahel
An area in Africa that is just south of the Sahara and tends to be fairly dry and hot.

TO LEARN MORE

BOOKS

Batten, Mary. *Life in Hot Water: Wildlife at the Bottom of the Ocean.* Atlanta: Peachtree, 2021.

Kington, Emily. *Deserts.* Truro, UK: Hungry Tomato, 2021.

Wilson, Libby. *Rattlesnakes.* Mendota Heights, MN: Apex Editions, 2023.

ONLINE RESOURCES

Visit **www.apexeditions.com** to find links and resources related to this title.

ABOUT THE AUTHOR

Ashley Gish has authored more than 60 juvenile nonfiction books. She earned her degree in creative writing from Minnesota State University, Mankato. Ashley lives in Minnesota with her husband and daughter.

INDEX

A
Australia, 20–21

C
camels, 13

D
Death Valley, 4, 7
desert spadefoots, 20

H
hydrothermal vents, 22, 24–26

J
jackrabbits, 19
jerboas, 10

L
Lut Desert, 14, 19

R
rattlesnake, 6, 8
roadrunners, 6, 8–9
Rüppell's foxes, 19
Rüppell's vultures, 13

S
Sahara, 10, 13
Sahel, 13
sand cats, 16
Sonoran Desert, 14

Y
yeti crabs, 26–27

ANSWER KEY:
1. Answers will vary; 2. Answers will vary; 3. C; 4. B; 5. B; 6. B